Catapult

A Journey Within

Corinne Van Meter

.

DEDICATION

To the voice that speaks when I listen and to all my fellow mystics
who encouraged me to share it . .

CONTENTS

Catapult (January 4, 2014 at Snow Canyon State Park)

I walk my path upward turning to see where I have been
searching for the road I've taken to ensure my safe journey home
but then the red rocks beckon me
to climb higher to sit among them
so I climb up, up
not afraid but with courage and wisdom
I AM this strength
I AM this majesty
I, too, AM part of
that which invites me into its circle
so I climb higher
to a seat where I now rest
it has been prepared for me by time
it invites me to stop
reflect
feel its strength
know it
the towering columns of red rock hug me with comfort
the medicine of the creosote nearby tells me
healing power is beside me
I need never fear
a fly plays in the coils of my notebook
then rests in the warmth of the golden light
the sun paints on my red jacket
I remain hidden in this landscape
yet I know where
I AM
I hear the shouts, the laughter, the struggle
of those who also climb
who walk the paths below where I AM
but I sit in my stillness
and feel the reward of my journey
I AM a bird flying into the face of the sun
and I AM joy . . .

On Questions

Source

Does the Sun know it is the Sun
perhaps one day it spread its rays
out into space
and felt its fullness
and experienced its light
radiating in all directions
growing larger and larger
sensing the space around itself
playing in its creation
feeling its light shining
in all places
into all things
spreading itself into hidden corners
of space and time
so there was no beginning
and no end
just the Sun
perhaps the Infinite Rays
from the thought of the Creator Sun
played on in their space
radiating their light
creating, feeling, experiencing
and when they looked to see
the Source
from which they had come
they saw only
the brilliant light of the Sun
upon which they could not gaze
but a moment
for they were blinded
by their Source's greatness
the light from which they had come
and which they are . . .

The Question of God

What is God you ask
God is All that Is
God Is
God Is in the Knowing of
That Which Is
God Is in the Knowing of
That Which Is Not
The Is Not Is, is it not
in the beginning Was
The All, The Is
and It expanded Itself
growing, creating Is Not
Duality where We live
where God experiences
through Us
The Is Not
Where is God you ask
hiding Its Knowingness
In All
Everywhere in Everything
Forever for Always
in All Ways
in the never-ending
Knowing of All
the In, the Out
the Up, the Down
the Forward, the Backward
the Seen, the Unseen
the Action, the Stillness
the Spoken, the Unspoken
in All God's Creation
God Is within Knowing
waiting to be found
remembered
in Its Journey in Our Now
when You find Knowing
You find God
maybe . . .

The Perfection of Creation

All the little moments of my life
constructed, assembled
pieced together in a pattern
meant for who I Am
in this vehicle I wear
to maneuver through
the time and space
which is my life
here in duality
where I temporarily dwell
inside the illusion
inside the form of all thought
I Am a piece of my Creator's Creation
Its perfect thought
moving freely
yet secretly created
by the mind of the Source of All
I, too, Am a Creator
can I be without judgment
of my Creation
can I feel gratitude
for the perfection of
all the parts which surround Me
that *are* Me as I journey
in this experience called life
can I love Myself
as I Am . . .

Mirrors

What if the only mirror
on this earth
was found in your eyes
I'd finally see myself
who I AM
life's truth
inside your eyes
so many mirrors
so many reflections
light bouncing
from me to you
from you to me
every moment
until we'd balance
then blend
into knowing
we are
ONE . . .

Creations

Each and every creation existing on
and surrounding this earth
be it great or small
serves a purpose in the design of life
as does every stitch in a tapestry
every brushstroke in a painting
why then is it so hard to accept that
every thought we have
every choice we make
every feeling we sense
every happening that occurs
every relationship we share
every person we meet
each one is necessary
to the design of our lives
our creation
and why
when we look to the sky with its sun
and its moon
and its planets
and its billions
and billions of stars
can we not see
something still greater exists . . .

Sacrifice

Are there those among us
who give their lives as sacrifice
to leave for us a treasure
that expands our life
to help us understand
something we must know
through an opportunity freely given
that helps our soul to grow
the innocent
an accident
perhaps a choice
sacrifices of love
calls from the
Divine voice

maybe being human weakens
when the soul comes a calling
maybe Spirit knows its promise
no questions
no stopping
no looking back
no wondering
it has done its perfect work
then it takes its leave
to places unseen
to view its handiwork

the tapestry of the soul
cannot be seen
it's a weaving of beauty
beyond all understanding
in our journey
through this life
over questions
we will surely trod
but in silence
we can leave the judging
to God . . .

Dark to Light

If you ask me
how do I change the dark to light
I say
go to the light that burns inside of you
feel it
and your darkness will dissolve
I cannot take you there
it is you who must decide to make the journey
on your own
in your way
in your time
choose to stop what you are being
quiet your mind
close your eyes to the distraction
the illusion
breathe
Be stillness
listen
live only in this moment
notice your presence
your Being in this place
feel the energy of who you are
in this visit with your Source
know that you are always this
at all times
listen to the wee small voice
that beckons you to rise above
all around you
listen to it tell you
that you are stronger
more powerful than anything
any problem
any feeling
that you are experiencing
you are in control of
all you allow yourself to be
it has been your choice all along

it remains your choice
take time to remember
God lives in all of your Beingness
whatever it may BE
and All Is well . . .

On Being Human

An Unlocked Prison

Vessels

The Dance of Relationship

Shape

Challenge Overcome

A Disappointment

A Hurt

Return to Love

An Unlocked Prison
. . . inspired by Marco

Are you stuck behind a prison door
impossible to escape
in a windowless fortress of mortar and stone
that you cannot seem to break

To rattle the door is futile
to yell to rant to rave
why me brings nothing more to you
but misery suffering pain

Stop breathe make it beautiful
this place where your Spirit lies
something waits in your stillness
as you go deep inside

Open the door to your heart
and you can journey in
to find your truth your own light
for peace lies within

The bird of Hope waits for you there
so climb upon its wings
and soar to the heights in the open air
transforming this space you are in

No cares are there where he takes you
outside those prison walls
know the I AM of your being
once here you cannot fall

The key to your freedom is with you
it has been there all along
just go inside of your heart
to hear the bird's sweet song . . .

Vessels

If it is that we are vessels
then it is that we are teachers
for each other
Knowing the lessons
without knowing them
really
Being them instead
letting them flow out
into the world . . .
what a gift that is
to us
to be channels of God's energy
as It circles in Its Knowing
within this illusion
in this moment
in time
how exciting it is to BE
when we are awake
and see . . .

The Dance of Relationship

We somewhere made
a secret vow
we'd help each other
in our Now
so why is it
I fight you so
if I'd just Be
my soul would grow

Sometimes our tasks
can make us weep
but still the promise
is ours to keep
others may judge
they do not know
the plan we made
so long ago

Perhaps they do
and play their part
they too were there
from the start
like an endless circle
our lives connect
in a dance of secrets
promises kept

If we only knew
that it was so
we could banish fear
life's great foe
freedom joy
and love could reign
doesn't that
change the game . . .

Shape

My body is a carrying case
for the Great I AM
can I see I am in control of it
it is separate from
who I really AM
it is a reflection of my creation
my experiences
why do I allow its form
to steal my power
hold me back
stop me
with its blocked energy
I can release what binds
my body and my mind
with thoughts of
my Spirit
empty allows room
for the Now
for the excitement
of the dream
let me clear my body
so that my journey
may be lightened
and I may
dance with joy
unencumbered
along its pathways . . .

Challenge Overcome

You are
as a newborn child
and yet
a woman of wisdom
floating on
your ocean of challenge
the thunderous wave
that carried you
to places so deep
so hidden
has quieted
you are awake
forever changed
eyes opened to see
the stars
the sun
the moon
beyond yourself
you have journeyed
inside of your being
and now float
upon the waters
relaxing emotion
becoming the waves
feeling a freedom
you would never know
had the darkness
not come
it has made you whole . . .

A Disappointment

Something happened
that I hadn't planned
and changed everything
that I thought would be
now I am feeling
abandoned
confused
lost
I allow myself
to feel them
then I awake
to a different place
a new space of Being
Knowing that
it may Be
the best part of my plan
the one that will lead me
to a higher place
truth comes
and I feel gratefulness
Divine plans overshadow
the temporary ones
I smile once more
and sing my song
humming the tune
in another direction . . .

A Hurt

Just when I think I'm past it all
when I've conquered that foe inside
you speak a word and it sends me back
into that pit so wide
I feel it first in the core of me
I've strived to feel it no more
but it rears its ugly head to me
poking through a fragile door
why should some words hurt me
they were yours just a short time ago
those words you speak bounce back to you
but still they pain me so
I remain meek almost succeed
then it does surprise me
that I have taken them into my heart
and I try to set them free
I open the cage to let them fly
into the sky above
and replace them with a newborn bird
a bird whose name is Love . . .

Return to Love

Here I am on an endless road
standing in this place with a choice
I can turn left
I can turn right
one way leads to darkness
the other to light
in this moment I choose the dark
I feel cold
I cannot see
I am lost
alone
behind me shines the light
It beckons me to turn into Its warmth
to feel It bathe me in Its love
I turn
I AM never lost
for the light knows the fire in me
and It never forgets . . .

On Lessons

The Wisdom of Forgiveness

Judgment

Grace

Understanding

Karma

Searching for Beauty

The Secret

The Wisdom of Forgiveness

Do you not yet know
that forgiveness
is a gift to yourself
a word or a deed
has no meaning to you
except what you hold
inside the core of you
due to its happening
and your judgment of it
to truly forgive another
we must release ourselves
from that which holds us
down in the water
and threatens to drown us
memories of resentment
weave a chain
which weighs us down
and we fall
as a caged bird
sinking within a sea
unable to breathe
unable to fly

Let the links of the chains
that bind you
be dissolved by the love
that surrounds you
so you may spread your wings
rise to the sky and soar
to the highest heights
and so it is
that to forgive another
is to liberate ourselves
go now
set yourself
and your brother free . . .

Judgment

I do not judge you
I cannot condemn you
For you are your Father's Child
Made in His image
All Powerful
All Present
All Feeling
How can I name a grievance
Are you not
God's thought
The Creator's voice
Are you not made from
His freedom to create
So, I, as well am free
As you are also free
To be that which you choose
I can then choose to see
The Spark which resides
In your beingness
And honor it
As I honor that
Which is also in me
Is it not so
That we are one . . .

Grace

What is grace
I've often tried
to capture it in words
for me it remains illusive
like words I've not yet heard
but to my heart
she does speak
in moments constantly
she washes me clean
like a gentle rain
on a fresh spring day
makes my Spirit lightly dance
as a butterfly at play
she kisses my cheek
and holds me close
when solace I do seek
she offers understanding
in whispers mild and meek
she cradles me in compassion
she sings in her voice Divine
she tells me she loves me
forever for all time
my heart knows her
that's what counts
in this life of mine
I need no words
my heart is clothed
in Grace's raiment fine . . .

Understanding

The part which is the Whole
the One which is
the Sum of all its parts
the One from which
all Its parts have come
sees the value
in each of Its parts
no judgment
how can we then
judge ourselves
for we are all of our parts
as we also are a part of
the Whole which does not judge
my Spirit lives
in a never-ending
perpetual design of creation
all is well indeed
for I AM
a part of the
Great I AM
and peace can be found
in that knowing . . .

Karma

Karma
is not punishment
to be feared
but the soul's craving
to balance
Its cosmic story
in agreement
in the world of duality
in a game called
Experiencing The Illusion of Life
an endless game
even games played within the game
until a time out
then we regroup change places
and a new game begins
just games played in moments
in this place called earth
a perpetual stream of Being
to BE
experienced
enjoyed
in peace
for no matter how this game goes
there is another one to be played
we've just forgotten . . .

Searching for Beauty

The kind of beauty you seek
cannot be seen
it must be felt with the heart
it is the heart that leads you
to the vibration of the soul
where the truth of beauty lies
it can be found
in the passion of the flowers
the song of the bird
the dance of the light
that is within all of
earth's creations and experiences
you have been striving to find it
by examining life
through the microscope in your head
but the lesson my friend is
it must be experienced
your soul knows it
your soul knows truth
when YOU experience NOW
you will find beauty
you will be satisfied
and your questions will fall away
you will BE LOVE
for that is what you really are
what we all are
LOVE seeking to remember itself
in a maze of diversion
when you finally see the beauty
of that which is not
balance will come
and you will know peace
just keep Being . . .

The Secret

And so it is that
the Creator loves Its Creation
without condition
without judgment
and the Creation continues
to create for the Creator
Being the Creator Itself
but living in Its blindness
always seeking
to know Its beginning
that which Is inside of Itself
the Is
the Was
the Always Will Be
which Is waiting to be felt
to Be experienced
to Be known
and so It Is indeed . . .

On Self

I Am All That Is

Return

Journey of the Light

Silence

Shadow

Finding Stillness

Fog

Meditating

I Am All That Is

I Am never separated from Anything
Anything is God
All is God
All is the Source of my Being
I need not ever fear Anything
for I AM All in human form
I have come to this place
to know it while I am Being here
feelings are ways of Being
I AM not them
they are waves on the ocean inside this jar
where I in a moment choose to live
my Soul knows this
I have been on an ageless journey
to knowing in this physical form
this time I try to know faster more quickly
so I can radiate my light my healing light
into the world around me
that others may shine more quickly more brightly
and our light may unite to raise this world around us
into a place of peace of understanding of knowing
We are Everything
Everything is Us
We are ONE
the embodiment of the Living Christ
who in His last journey in this realm
showed us who We Are
demonstrated the secret of our Being
revealed the truth of our existing
We live
in all time
in all space
for always
He has whispered the secret into our hearts
to be unlocked by us and only us
in our own way in our own time
that is our journey
ours alone . . .

Return

I am as a fluffy white cloud
floating in an endless sea of blue
so light so airy so peaceful
full of joy without form
empty yet full
I have risen past the highest mountain top
past the blackness of space
into the full color of love which surrounds me
and lifts me still higher and higher yet
into the place called eternity
where All is known
into the presence of the Great I AM

I seek reconnection for my next mission
in my journey of moving forward
I am here along with other clouds
knowing they too are floating
being each a part of the All
of which I too Am a part

We touch for brief moments
then gently bounce to one another
and I smile in a new way
for we are bliss together
no judgment
no anticipation
just being
moving freely
floating in love
complete
connected
light expanded
parts merged
once again
I AM ONE . . .

Journey of the Light

I am inside of a barn
there is a crack in the battered board
where a beam of light is streaming
a small hole of light but still it illuminates
outside shines the sun
seeking to brighten the space inside
with a tiny stream of light
now I must be here trying to see
what I am searching for
and if I stand a certain way
change my perspective
use the little light inside this space
I can find what I am looking for
the light I see inside this barn
will grow in time for the sun outside
will overtake these fading walls
they will crumble and fall
to reveal an open space
a place once hidden
by man's desiring to create a space
to shelter some earthly illusions
and hide them from the light
but the light in its truth
always shines in the darkness
and it always wins

Am I this little light
living in the darkened space
I've created inside of my barn
somewhere outside
the eternal light of God
enfolding me
protecting me
loving me
always doing its perfect work
wearing away the structure I've made

to house my beam of light
will it continue to illuminate my shadows
exposing me revealing
who I really am
is not the light of the All
stronger than that which it embraces
our walls are only temporary
they don't really exist
only the thought of them
the light of truth
will dissolve those facades
then humanity will know
we are all part of God . . .

Silence

I am so grateful for this silence
I am not afraid of the stillness
as perhaps I once was
I have grown to need
its companionship
to walk with it
rest with it
listen to it speak to me
ever so softly within me
God is in that silence of mine
it is God that is my partner
I have found the indwelling Christ
the Source of All
inside of me
how can I not be grateful
each moment I live
each moment I breathe
whatever befalls me
on my journey here
I know
the Creator walks with me
loving me
guiding me
speaking in my silence
and I am grateful indeed . . .

Shadow

I AM darkness
for I AM being darkness
living for this moment
in shadow
a moment that seems so long
but I can choose at any time
to be something else
to feel something else
to change what I AM being
just a simple switch of my thought
that opens the door
starts the dominoes falling
taking my being
in a different direction
helping me climb up
to a new place
this mind of mine
can do amazing things
it can turn darkness to light
suffering to joy
I AM
filled with possibility . . .

Finding Stillness

I close my eyes
and notice my breath
life's breath
sustaining me
in the place
where my Spirit dwells
I cannot stop
the world around me
but I can go
inside of me
and search
for my resting point
here too
I cannot stop
the thoughts
inside my head
so I choose
to see
the space
in between them
the stillness
that holds
the thought
I rest here
noticing
just noticing
and soon
the stillness
grows
around me
and
in this place
I AM
finding rest
in my
now . . .

Fog

It is strange that today
I see a thick fog outside my window
I cannot see my world's familiar picture
only a thick blanket
blocking everything from my view
limited cut-off unsure
a perfect reflection of me now
at this moment I allow myself
to feel the frustration of confinement
being strapped down
my hands and legs unable to move
I am lost in it
now I choose to open my eyes
to focus on what surrounds me
I can still see I can still move freely
in this small space where I Am
without fear of what I cannot see
here is where I must be for now
living enclosed in a mist
which appears to block the light
which always is
for without the light behind the fog
I could not see at all
soon the sun will burn the curtain away
and the radiance of the light
will reveal itself
I will bask in its warmth and my soul will delight
for it knew the light was there all along . . .

Meditating

As I climb to higher heights
past my mind
into my soul's expansiveness
I feel the light which I AM
I float in freedom within an open sky
glimpsing the alpha and omega
of my being
far from the illusory life I live
in the space called earth
no distractions
no whirling energies
to divert me
I bask
in the solace
in the silence
in the loneliness
in the fullness surrounding me
I AM peace
and all is well . . .

On Life

Life

I am walking on a pathway toward the light
in the distance are clouds past them is the All
I am focused on the mystery before me
but for now I must be on the road where I AM
surrounded by doors that invite me
to explore what's behind them
I stop momentarily peering inside some of them
sometimes I willingly step within for a while
other times I walk on by
some doors are wide open and it seems
an invisible hand pulls me into a frenzy
there is always the door of escape present
to lure me inside where I sleep in its nothingness
doors all around me
behind each one a world of feelings
excitement surprise sadness pain
compassion joy anger understanding
either love or fear
sometimes I just stand on the road
and spin turning in confusion
but when I finally stop I recognize
I am still on the road
moving closer to my destination
the doors I have chosen to enter
have filled me with strength and wisdom for my journey
experiencing all of it
balancing myself within it is what I came here to do
when all the doors of this life are closed to me
I will walk freely to the light with no regret
for each step I took each door I opened
was perfect for me
each one brought me closer to
Who I AM . . .

The Beauty of Aging

We come to this world
along with lifetimes of experiences
we choose new life
to BE once again
in this maze of 'reality'
finding our way back to knowing
it is seeing from the Soul
that brings us to recognize
the worth of each season
the perfection of its timing
our life here and now
is but a thread
in Our Divine tapestry
a masterpiece of exquisite beauty
growing larger
and more magnificent
throughout the ages
and spaces of time
expanding as the wonder of
the All . . .

The Spark

The spark lives in you resides in your being
like the burning embers of a smoldering fire
it can be brought to new life
 into dancing columns of flame
it can burn strong and bring warmth and light

The fire that burns inside your being is the truth
the light the spark of the Living Christ
always there in all time in all circumstance
ready to ignite with love just now resting

Embers shining brightly in the darkness
waiting to grow waiting to be fanned
so that the light in you may become brighter
and overshadow the darkness that hides

It never stops burning
for the eternal light of God always is
and its flame lives on in you forever . . .

A Journey Song

Perhaps my road was a Divine plan
put together by my own hand
it has been my choice all along
a chance to sing a journey song
to enjoy the ride along the way
see me in you just a game to play
needless struggle needless fear
all around always near
but I can choose another way
to see beauty in each new day
see my now every moment I live
see the gift of wisdom it gives
let it be revealed before my eyes
take off my mask no longer hide
to the knowing of Who I AM
experiencing myself was always the plan
and when this small journey on earth is through
I release myself to rest and renew
and know myself in light's highest bliss
and all the universes my greatness kiss . . .

The Game

The Spirit in this body
has come to play a game
within its reflection
to play a game
of seeming chance
seeking all experience
a game played
neither won nor lost
scores are only judgments
there are other games
to be played
NOW
play your game
with abandon
in freedom
enjoy the twists
and turns
of your creation
as a bird
flying free
through the open sky
following its compass
singing its song
being joy
soaring
spreading light
in each moment
playing in
the beauty of the game . . .

The Way It Is

I sit and watch the wispy white clouds
hang gently in the sky
their beauty draws me to them
it catches my examining eye
on another day they may billow in puffs of cottony fluff
I play inside this wonder I cannot get enough
sometimes they will intrigue me when they gather
brushed with black
soon comes refreshment from the rain
blue skies will then come back
are all of those clouds like events in my life
passing over *my* earth
drifting freely through *my* light
do I recognize their worth
can I look at my clouds with more clarity
and see them as merely experiences for me
to learn and grow and fill my days while I'm here
inside this shell as my truth appears
can I see past the clouds to the light in my skies
and know that inside me all answers lie
find love in my heart find peace in my soul
know that each cloud has indeed made me whole
can I sit without judgment as my clouds have their way
allow them to be and inside them just play . . .

ABOUT THE AUTHOR

Corinne Van Meter is a teacher and an inspirational writer and speaker. She is the author of *Is it Dusk or Is it Dawn: A Hopeful Journey Through Grief* and the award-winning children's book *The Little Girl Who Wanted to Fly: The Incredible True Story of Vicki Van Meter*. She has inspired audiences across the country with stories of her life-changing personal experiences, as well as interpretations of her poetry and now shares those mystical connections in her new book *Catapult.*

She lives on a mountain top in St. George, Utah along with Jim, her husband of forty-six years, and their dogs; Maya and Tiffany, but she retreats to North Carolina in the spring to write and reflect. She is the mother of three; Elizabeth, Daniel, and Victoria and the grandmother of one; Lukas.

To contact Corinne, visit her website: www.ananchoroflight.com

www.ingramcontent.com/pod-product-compliance
Lightning Source LLC
Chambersburg PA
CBHW060136050426
42448CB00010B/2151